Freestyle Swimming

ALSO BY DR. FRANK RYAN

Weight Training

High Jump

Pole Vault

Sprint

THE VIKING LIBRARY OF SPORTS SKILLS

FREESTYLE SWIMMING

DR. FRANK RYAN

NEW YORK / THE VIKING PRESS

Author's Note

Freestyle Swimming, another addition to the Viking Library of Sports Skills, is published in connection with the teaching sound film, "Sprint Crawl." This film now has sound tracks in five languages and is being enthusiastically used throughout most of the world by thousands of coaches and millions of swimmers. Scenes from the film are reproduced in this book.

When the film was being produced, we asked Phil Moriarty, Varsity Swimming Coach at Yale University, to be our chief consultant. Coach Moriarty, one of America's famous swim coaches, has extraordinary qualifications. A professional coach since 1932, Phil has had wide and intensive experience in all phases of aquatics. In 1960 he was United States Men's Olympic diving coach, and in 1965 he was head coach of the U. S. Maccabiah swimming team.

During Coach Moriarty's twelve years as head varsity coach at Yale, his swim teams have lost only three of 149 dual meets. In the Eastern Intercollegiate Swim League Moriarty's teams have won nine championships and tied for another. Yale has captured the Eastern Seaboard Championship for the past eight years. Phil's teams have been second in the AAUs six times and twice in the NCAA championships.

Phil Moriarty has coached world-record holders, Olympians, and many other greats. However, equally impressive is his work in teaching swimming to thousands of young people. In addition to his Yale coaching duties,

vii

Phil has, during the summers, been the swimming instructor at the St. Louis Country Club. Thousands of his young pupils have become more proficient swimmers, and some have gone on to greatness.

Coach Moriarty's teaching approach combines the best features of nearly forty years of experience with a fresh point of view. He is constantly alert for new and more effective methods and approaches.

Though we have leaned heavily on Phil's views, the responsibility for the contents of this book must rest with the author.

Preface

Modern swimming techniques have had a remarkably short history. Presently used styles are the products of very recent times. Today's competitive swimmers would look strikingly different from even the champions of the early part of this century. In contrast, the distance runner of today would resemble the runner of ancient times.

It is appropriate to compare swimming and running. They have borrowed much from each other in formulating conditioning views. By now their training methods are quite similar.

All parts of the earth are covered by either land or water. Without mechanical aid, or strictly on his own, man has the potential of movement on land or through the water. The words *on* land and *through* water are significant. Man does move *through* water—not *on* it. That's because the specific gravity of the human body is very close to that of water. This fact has no doubt had an enormous influence on the story of man and the water. The story would have been different if all men had great natural buoyancy —and different again if nobody could float. As things are, man's actions in the water are critical. They decide whether he sinks or swims.

Even though three-quarters of the earth's surface is covered by water, man has been primarily a creature of the land. More than a billion people have lived and died without having swum a single stroke. Even today, many millions of people cannot swim. Yet every able-bodied person can move about the land by walking or running.

It seems puzzling that it took mankind so long to develop efficient swimming techniques. You would think that man would have learned to swim well even before he learned to speak or develop a culture. The water was always there for him.

Much of the explanation for man's early failure to swim proficiently probably lies in the nature of a good part of the surrounding water. A lot of the water is rough, cold, or otherwise dangerous. However, in certain parts of the world the waters are ideal for inducing man to enter them. Not only are the conditions for swimming good, but there are tangible rewards in the forms of fish and shellfish. The ideal spots seem to be in the South Seas Islands.

The South Seas Islanders were rewarded in their food-seeking efforts in the surrounding waters. In addition, the fun-loving and relaxed temperament of the natives played a part. They enjoyed the activity of swimming and became good at it. They actually developed a form of the crawl stroke.

The next link in the historic chain came about because of the nearness of Australia to the Islands. Possibly the most sporting people in the world, the Australians were especially fond of swimming. The Australian swimmers observed the methods of the islanders. They then adopted and refined what they saw. The swimming revolution had started.

The roots were there, but three more contributions were needed to bring swimming performance to its present level. First, smooth water is necessary for highly efficient speed swimming. Open water is simply too rough. The construction of well-engineered pools has been a critical part of modern swimming history. Happily, more and more pools are being built.

Second, there has been the emergence of professional swimming coaches. Able and dedicated, these men spent countless hours in improving their sport. All phases of swimming were constantly analyzed. They looked especially to the physical sciences to yield refinements and ideas on the mechanics of swimming. Within this framework they carried on bold and fruitful experiments.

Third, swimming has been participating in a "conditioning revolution" that has been affecting all sports. Until about a generation ago our training schedules were based largely on intuition and guesswork. It turned out that we badly underestimated the optimum amounts of work. Physiological research has drastically revised our notions of what a workout should be.

Swimming is an exciting sport. Its progress in the past fifty years outstrips the advances made in the previous million years. The application of modern science and thinking has made the difference. But, first and foremost, swimming is a sport—and it's fun. Perhaps no other sports activity is more rewarding to the participant.

Contents

Freestyle Swimming

Approach to Form

In a freestyle race you can, by definition, use any style that you want. If you liked you could begin with one stroke and switch to another during the race. But, as a practical matter, you would stay entirely with the crawl stroke, because it is the fastest stroke yet devised.

What is good sprint-crawl form? How do we judge it? By good form we mean the use of the body and its parts to move through the water as efficiently as possible. Hence there should really be nothing mysterious about good form. In general, our notions of good form derive from two bases—experience and theory. Many new techniques have been tried by coaches and swimmers over the generations. The innovations that seemed to work well have been retained and used. Others have been discarded. So some of our present teachings were evolved by trial and error. We profit from the experience of countless swimmers.

As in many other athletic events, our present ideas of swimming form have been shaped by theoretical considerations including physical principles. We can deduce points that seem likely to offer improvement. When both practical experience and theory are in agreement, we can have a high level of confidence in our views.

Let's approach the problem of sprint crawl in a simple and systematic way. Suppose we consider a model (photo series 1) that could represent any floating body. If this body is to move through the water, what factors will determine its speed? How fast our model will move depends upon

3

(photo #1a) its power plant, (photo #1b) the amount of resistance that the body offers to the water, and (photo #1c) the efficiency of propulsion.

If we think in terms of a boat, we can easily visualize each of the three factors that affect speed. Other things equal, a boat with a high-powered engine will move faster than one with less power. But the engine has to be in good condition. Otherwise, it won't make the contribution to speed that it should.

Resistance always exists whenever a body moves through the water. A boat's bow has to push water aside. Its stern tends to drag water with it. Some resistance is inevitable, but marine engineers try to design boats so that this resistance is reduced as much as possible.

Efficiency of propulsion is the remaining factor in determining speed. Power should be applied so that it best brings about forward movement. It is possible to use enormous power without getting much propulsion from it. In fact, poor use of power could cause the body to remain motionless or even move backward.

What applies to all floating bodies generally applies to the swimmer. He conditions his "power plant." He must be strong and in excellent physical condition. He tries for a streamline body position that will minimize water resistance. He learns swimming techniques that will propel him efficiently. Swimming, however, does have a realistic complication. Unlike the boat, the swimmer must use a substantial part of his body for propulsion. In other words, for the swimmer the reduction of body resistance and the efficiency of propulsion are related. Some streamlining has to be sacrificed to get better propulsion.

1. A body's speed through the water depends upon (1a) its power plant, (1b) the resistance it offers to the water, (1c) the efficiency of propulsion.

1a

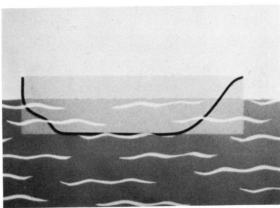

1b

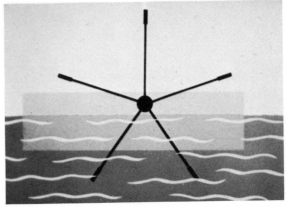

1c

Body Position

The less resistance that your body offers to the water the faster you will move. The human body isn't very streamlined compared to that of a fish, but there is still a lot that we can do to lessen drag. Body position in the water can have great effect on the amount of resistance.

Let's suppose that you are holding on to a rope and being towed through the water at a constant speed. As you assume different body positions you would feel different amounts of pull or pressure on the rope. The amount of pull you felt would indicate the amount of drag your body was creating. The greatest resistance would be felt with your body in a vertical position. The least resistance would occur when your body becomes straight and flat.

You can see that you'll move best when your body lies in a flat position. The body should be almost parallel to the surface of the water. Your body cannot be completely parallel, however, because your feet have to be deep enough to kick effectively. The head and chest are a little higher than the lower body. The position of the head puts the hairline about even with the surface of the water. The head is comfortably held in alignment with the body. The shoulders are at right angles to the line of the body.

Training in correct breathing starts at the poolside. You learn to bob up and down taking a deep breath above the water and then to drop below the water to force out the air. The bobbing up and down is carried out with an easy rhythm. Most of the time is spent under water in expiration.

6

The ratio is about five to one—that is, for every second that the head is above the surface it is submerged for about five seconds.

Inhalation is through the mouth. And it is rapid. There just isn't much time to take in a breath. You breathe out through both your nose and mouth. Though you have to inhale quickly, there is much more time to exhale. Air can be expelled smoothly and easily.

You can breathe without lifting your head. You can put yourself into position to breathe with an easy twisting of your neck. The reason you can do this is that the head creates a bow wave. The water is pushed aside, and there is a trough or "hole" in the water. The head rotates smoothly so that a breath can be taken at the bottom of the depression. In this way the head doesn't have to be lifted very much, and there is only a slight interference with streamlined body position. Rotation of the head is the key to efficient breathing. Rotation serves two purposes. The head does not have to be lifted, and the body does not have to be turned.

The rotation of the head need not and certainly should not be forced or artificial. The rotation should be smoothly and easily coordinated with body rotation. During each stroke the body has a natural tendency to roll to one side. The head should roll in the same direction.

In the short sprint races very few inhalations are needed. A trained sprinter can swim a full pool length with only several breaths. In the longer races it is common practice to take in a breath with every second stroke.

After starting, it is best that no breaths be taken during the first few strokes. This is the time when good body position is established. If the head does not have to be turned, a streamlined body position is easier to attain.

The first approach to getting good body position is to visualize it—to have a clear picture and then to try directly for it. This is the positive way. However, it's realistic to know that the body can get out of alignment along any one of three axes, even if it is straight. When we speak of these three possibilities for error we mean that (1) the body could fail to be flat enough, (2) the body could be sideways, and (3) the body could be rolling too much. Let's look at each.

Of the three possible errors the most common is the failure to maintain a level position in the water. Usually this comes from trying to lift the head too high with a resulting dropping of the lower body. In most cases this error can be eliminated by emphasis on correct breathing habits. Failure to kick sufficiently can also drop the lower body. We'll be talking about this when we get to the subject of leg action.

A swinging of the body from side to side increases water resistance or drag. This lateral movement can have a number of roots. Movement of the head out of alignment will tend to drive the body sideways. Correct arm action is essential to keeping good body position. Lateral movement of the arms tends to produce lateral movement of the body. Though any phase of the stroke may contribute to poor body alignment, lateral motion seems to be more common during recovery. Many swimmers have difficulty swinging their arms in a vertical plane. This error usually comes from lack of flexibility. Special exercises may be needed.

The legs have a strong effect on body alignment. Their action on the downbeat overcomes the tendency on the lower body to sink. In this way the legs help keep the body flat. But leg action also greatly influences lateral alignment. Faulty kicking could throw the body from side to side, but for the most part leg action tends to preserve alignment. The legs almost automatically kick slightly sideways to compensate for lateral forces introduced by the arms or head.

A rolling about the long axis of the body increases water resistance. Though a completely stable body position would produce less drag, a certain amount of roll is both inevitable and needed. With a rolling motion the arms can pull more effectively, and breathing can be carried out easier. You should not make a direct effort to roll, but don't try to stop the roll either. Let it come naturally.

How *high* should you ride in the water? There seems to be considerable concern with this question, but not much can or should be done about it. Theoretically, the higher you are in the water the faster you will go, and, conversely, the faster you move the higher you will be in the water. However, at swimming speed the amount of lift that the body receives is not significant. Efforts to ride higher in the water are not only useless—they are damaging. Direct efforts to lift the body interfere with both alignment and efficient propulsion.

How high you swim depends primarily on your natural buoyancy. Muscle and bone are relatively heavy. Most fine sprinters are big-boned and heavily muscled. This means a high specific gravity. Hence many good sprinters cannot even float. So don't worry about your height in the water.

In summary, body position is a highly significant factor in swimming. Drag must be reduced as much as possible. You start by being aware of the

8

need for good position, and you try to visualize what this position should be. Nonalignment has to be checked along three axes—up and down, sideways, and extreme rolling. With increased experience your own feelings about the position of your body will become more and more reliable. You will get to feel or sense unnecessary water resistance. But, whenever possible, get the observations of your coach. Body position should be checked regularly. If needed, you and your coach can figure out the corrective action that should be taken.

2. A flat, streamlined body position cuts down water resistance. The legs are slightly lower than the upper body to permit effective kicking. Note (e and f) that the head turns so that breathing can be carried out without disturbing body position.

2d

2a

2e

2b

2f

2c

3. Poolside training in correct breathing. Breaths are taken quickly. Five times as much time is spent under water in exhaling.

4. Intake of air actually takes place in the trough or "hole" created by the bow wave.

3a

4

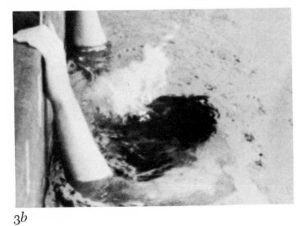

3b

Arms

The arms supply most of the forward propulsion. Some experts think that the arms supply all or nearly all of swimming power. This position is probably an extreme position, but the great importance of arm action is entirely clear. The arms are not as strong as the legs. The enormous contribution to forward movement made by the arms comes mainly from their flexibility, including the fact they can be taken out of the water during recovery. The flexibility of the arms permits much of their effort to be applied efficiently. We will be looking at this efficiency. During recovery the arms are brought back through the air rather than the water. For this reason there is greater arm speed, and much less water resistance is created.

All aspects of swimming are important to great performance, but if we had to single out one aspect as the most important, it would be arm action. This action must be efficient. It has to be understood, learned, and ingrained. Champions may have differences in some things they do, but all have good arm action. Their smooth and efficient strokes contrast sharply with the wild arm thrashings of the novice.

So that we can take a clear and logical look at the chief features of arm action, let's examine a simple model (photo series 6). We illustrate with a model of an old-fashioned paddle wheel. Actually, the hand and forearm act like a paddle.

In our model suppose we isolate one paddle and follow this single paddle through a cycle. We can then examine the effect on forward propulsion of various positions.

When the paddle first enters the water (photos 6a, b) its action is mostly downward, and therefore the reaction is mostly upward. The force supplies a lot of lift but very little forward power. So you can see that, at this point in the stroke, much of the power is being wasted.

As the stroke proceeds (photo 6c) the lifting action becomes less, and the forward drive is increased. Efficiency is improving.

At that point where the paddle is straight down (photo 6d), efficiency reaches its peak. Push is directly backward, and for this reason all force is directed forward.

Now as the paddle moves past the vertical (photo 6e), it begins to push upward as well as backward. While at this point there is still a good backward push, there is also an upward push. Much of the energy is used in driving the body downward. Toward the completion of the stroke the force exerted by the paddle causes the boat to be pulled downward. Power is wasted. Efficiency is low.

Our model shows what happens when we have a fixed or rigid paddle. Only a brief portion of the stroke can be highly efficient. There is much waste. But suppose we have a way of changing the shape of the paddle during its stroke. Suppose we have a joint that allows a substantial portion of the paddle to be bent. This ability to bend makes a big difference. Now look at the early portion of the stroke (photo 7a). The bending allows the action to be more directly backward and, therefore, the reaction to be more directly forward. The efficiency of the first part of the stroke is greatly increased. We can, in fact, by bending the paddle, maintain an effective forward force during most of the stroke (photo series 7a–d). We can take our paddle model and easily translate its action into what it means for swimming. We know at once that stiff arms will not be efficient in propelling the body through the water. We know that the arms will have to bend during the stroke, and we know that the amount of bend is going to depend on the part of the stroke.

As you move your arm through the water, you can control the angle made by your upper and lower arm. In other words, a bending of the elbow can put the forearm in a better position to push backward throughout all phases of the stroke. Also, you can control the angle formed by your wrist and hand. By adjusting this angle the hand can be kept perpendicular to the surface of the water throughout the greater part of the stroke.

13

In summary, the flexion of your elbow and that of your wrist is used to push the water as directly backward as possible. The more directly you can drive the water backward, the more efficiently you drive your body straight ahead.

There is still another reason for flexing the elbow during the early part of the pull. The lever arm is shortened. Mechanical advantage is increased and more force can be exerted against the water. This is the same principle that permits a car to start faster in low gear. During the first part of the stroke the elbow should be higher than the hand. In this way both power and efficiency of propulsion are greater.

Action and reaction are in opposite directions. The direction in which the hand pushes the water is of great importance, because the body tends to move in the opposite direction. That's why the hands should move directly backward as much as possible. In this way the reaction pushes the body forward. Deviations from backward action of the hands tend to move the body sideways.

Arm action is alternate, that is, one arm pulls while the other recovers. It is not enough for the arms to move parallel to the body. Alternate pulls could produce lateral motion. So the pulling action is not only in alignment with forward direction. It is also beneath the center of the body.

Ideally, the stroke should satisfy two main requirements. First, you try to push the water directly backward. You do this by adjusting the angle made by your upper and lower arm and the angle made by your wrist and hand. Second, the path of your hand is directly under your body's center of gravity. Because of the body's construction the hand does not actually travel backward in a straight line. The path of the hand tends to be somewhat circular. The hand crosses the center line of the body and then comes back.

Recovery. When the arm completes a stroke, it has to be brought back or to recover so that another stroke can be started. Action is continuous. As the hand leaves the water at the end of the stroke it is moving fast and in a circular path. It is circular because the hand has to move outward to clear the body. If the arm were straight back, it would take considerable energy and time to reverse the backward movement and get the arm moving forward again. The rotary movement is utilized so that the momentum can be retained.

During the early part of the recovery the elbow leads the way. The hand starts to catch up so that it is about even with the elbow when it reaches shoulder level. From that point on the hand accelerates in a natural and unrushed fashion so that it enters the water first. Upon entering the water the palm is downward and at an angle to the surface. The elbow is partly bent.

The path of the recovery should as much as possible be in the vertical plane. The action should be upward and forward rather than sideways and forward. A sideways recovery of the arm tends to move the body sideways, thus throwing the body out of alignment. If there is continued trouble in making the recovery in the vertical plane, it may be due to tightness. Special exercises to increase shoulder flexibility may be needed.

The recovery can and should be a relaxed and smooth movement. The energy that you use to bring your arm out of the water will usually be enough to keep the arm moving forward. Once the arm is out of the water you apply just enough energy to control its path. This gives you a chance to relax your arms and thus reduce fatigue.

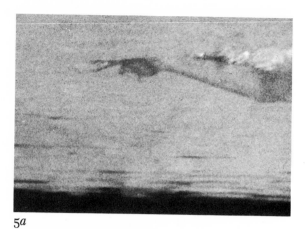

5a

5b

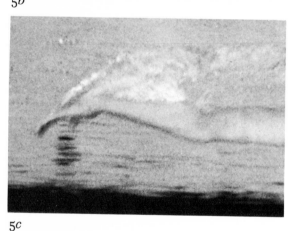

5c

5d

5. As the hand enters the water the wrist bends. In this way the hand can push backward.

6. A cycle of a straight paddle. When the paddle first enters the water (a) its action is almost entirely downward. Hence the reaction shown by the solid arrow (b) is upward. By (c) the reaction is in a more backward direction and therefore more efficient. At (d) where the paddle is pointed directly downward the stroke is most efficient. The entire action is backward. As the cycle continues (e), the action becomes increasingly inefficient. More and more the reaction is in a downward direction.

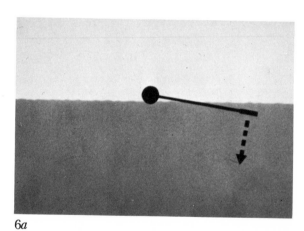

6a

6b

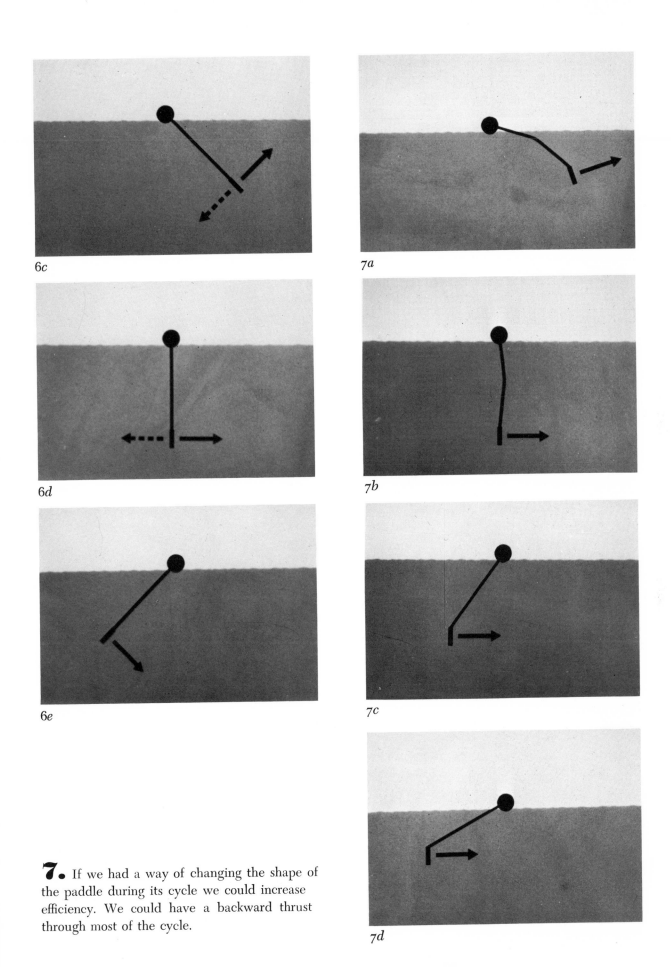

6c

6d

6e

7a

7b

7c

7d

7. If we had a way of changing the shape of the paddle during its cycle we could increase efficiency. We could have a backward thrust through most of the cycle.

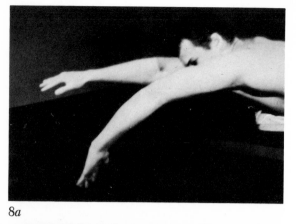

8a

8b

8. and **9.** Compare the dry-land series and the underwater sequence with the diagrams in series 7. By bending his elbows and wrists the swimmer greatly increases the efficiency of his arm action. He is able to push backward through much of the stroke.

9a

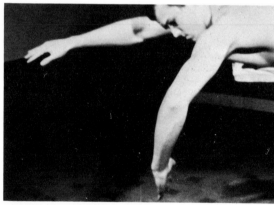

8c

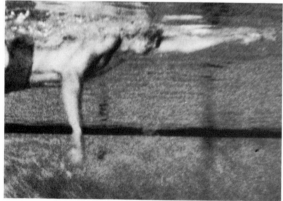

9b

8d

9c

10a

10b

10c

11a

11b

11c

11d

10. It's not enough for the stroke to be parallel to the body. The arms pull alternately. Action that is only parallel would drive the body from side to side (a and b). Hence the path of the stroke should be under the body.

11. The hand actually crosses the center line of the body. Its path is somewhat curved.

12a

12b

12c

12d

12.

13. Recovery. In (a) the elbow is leading the recovery. By (b) the lower arm has caught up to the upper arm. The forearm then goes ahead of the elbow (c). The recovery action is smooth, rhythmic, and relaxed. The initial action of pulling the arm out of the water should supply the momentum for the entire recovery.

13a

13b

13c

Legs

The legs, though stronger than the arms, contribute less to the forward propulsion of the body. Some coaches contend that the only function of the legs is to help stabilize the body. This position is extreme. It surely is theoretically and practically possible to derive forward propulsion from the kick. In fact, it is essential to get a contribution from the legs in order to do your best.

It's helpful to take a look at the theoretical problem of propulsion. For any part of the body to add to forward speed it must be moving *backward* through the water faster than the body is moving forward. Suppose we take a specific example. If the body is moving through the water at a rate of five feet per second, and, at the same time, a part of the body (the foot, for example) is moving backward in relation to the body at four feet per second, what is the situation? Though the part is moving backward in relation to the body, it is actually moving forward in relation to the water— and at a rate of one foot per second. Under this condition the part makes no contribution to forward movement. Quite the opposite. A drag is created.

Put another way, we have to make a distinction between "relative" and "absolute" movement. Suppose you are climbing a ladder in an elevator that is slowly descending. Assume that you are climbing at the rate of four feet per second and the elevator is going down at five feet per second. You would be going upward in relation to the elevator, but you would be going downward in relation to the earth. Your "absolute" speed is one foot per second in a downward direction—even though you are climbing. So it is with swimming. You could move your feet backward in a relative sense and not create propulsion. Movement of the feet has to be fast enough to be "absolute."

For the kick to be truly effective you have to build up to considerable backward foot speed. A distinction between "speed" and "force" is important. Actually, there can be force without any motion. You can push hard against a brick wall without moving it. In swimming it would be possible to apply tremendous force without contributing to propulsion. Speed has to be there too.

Even some of the experts have spread some confusion about the contribution of the kick. They reason as follows. If you swim with your legs tied you will move at a certain rate. This rate represents the contribution of the arms to speed. Now if you eliminate the arm action by using a kickboard, your legs will propel you forward, but at less speed than that of the arms alone. The false reasoning becomes this. If the arms can, for example, move the body forward at a speed of four feet per second and the legs move the body at two feet per second, the resulting speed has to be something like three feet per second. In this way the legs do more harm than good. But, of course, this is not necessarily so. It depends on how fast the feet are moving backward. If they can move backward faster than the arms alone can pull the body forward, then the kick makes a positive contribution. Total speed can be increased. The critical point is not centered about the speed at which the legs can drive a kickboard. It's a matter of how fast the feet can move backward.

In addition to speed, leg action has to be correct. In order to get a simple and rational view of what leg action should be, let's consider the up-and-down movement of a stiff leg (photo 15a). On the downward drive (photo 15b) the pressure on the water is partly down and partly backward. During this phase there is some forward component to the reaction (photo 15c).

At that point where the straight leg is parallel to the water's surface (photo 15d), the pressure is entirely downward. Hence the reaction is entirely upward (photo 15e). A lifting force is created, but there is no contribution to forward propulsion.

Toward the end of the downstroke (photo 15g) the reaction is upward and backward. There is a negative force or interference with forward propulsion.

On the upstroke of the leg the forces are reversed from those of the downstroke. During the first part of the upstroke, the reaction is forward and down (photo 15h). At the midpoint (photo 15i) the reaction is down only. Toward the end of the upstroke (photo 15j) the leg produces a force that is both backward and down.

If the legs were kept rigid their up-and-down movement would result in a cancellation of forces. Any forward force generated would be balanced by an equal backward force. There would, in fact, be a loss because of the drag produced. It is clear that stiff legs cannot contribute to forward propulsion.

We can analyze the above demonstration to see at what points forward propulsion is supplied. We note that there is forward power on the downstroke only before the leg reaches a horizontal position. We can say that on the downstroke there is a contribution to forward propulsion when the angle made by the leg and a horizontal line is greater than zero (photo 15k). Conversely, on the upbeat forward impetus is given to the body only when this angle is less than zero (photo 15l). So in order to get the legs to contribute to forward drive we want to reproduce these conditions. To do so one or more flexible joints are needed. Through flexibility the condition needed for forward propulsion can be met throughout the downstroke. Also, flexibility permits forward drive during the upstroke (photos 15m, n, o).

We can now see the importance of looseness, particularly a loose ankle. If the ankle is loose enough, pressure of the water against the ankle will automatically bring about the adjustments in the angle needed for propulsion. Looseness of the ankle will permit the foot to act as a flipper.

We have emphasized the ankle and foot. It's because the extremities of the limbs move faster. For example, if you swing your arm, your wrist and hand will move faster than your upper arm. The upper arm and muscles of the body supply nearly all of the power, but the speed is in the lower arm. In the same way, though the body and the upper legs supply the real power, what finally matters is the speed of the lower legs and feet.

Now we can summarize what the legs have to do. There are two big factors—speed and angle. The feet must move quickly, and they must push the water as directly backward as possible.

Leg action stabilizes. In addition to contributing to forward propulsion the legs have another important function—that of helping to keep the body stable. Their action aids in sustaining alignment and in keeping the body streamlined. It does so in both the vertical and lateral planes.

There is always a tendency for the lower part of the body to sink. The kick overcomes this dropping tendency and helps to preserve streamlining. The downbeat is a more powerful action than the upbeat. This greater pressure of the downward kick should develop enough force to keep the legs up.

The tendency for the body to move laterally or from side to side varies among swimmers. Much of the weaving can be counteracted by lateral action of the legs. This corrective, partially sideways thrust of the legs is usually carried out almost instinctively and without conscious effort. However, if excessive correction by the legs is needed, the upper body and arm action should be examined. They are introducing too much lateral action.

14. The kick serves two important purposes. It contributes to propulsion. Perhaps just as important, the kicking action helps stabilize the body and in this way it cuts down on drag.

14a

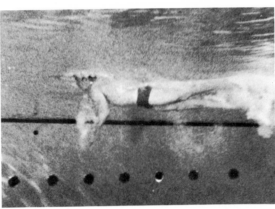

14c

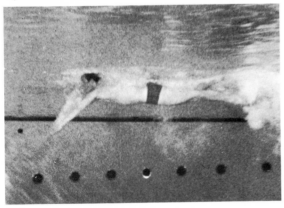

14b

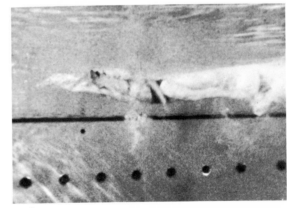

14d

15. Why stiff legs cannot contribute to propulsion. Assume we have two straight legs that move up and down (a). We isolate a single leg and follow its action to see what it does. In (b) the leg is starting downward. The dotted arrow shows the direction of the action. The reaction (solid arrow in c) is partly forward. There is some contribution to forward movement.

(d) Action is directly downward.

(e) Reaction is upward. There is a lifting action at this point.

(f) Downward past the vertical. Action is down and slightly forward.

(g) Reaction is upward, but also slightly backward.

(h, i, j) On the upward stroke the forces are reversed.

(k) On the downstroke forward impetus is given when the angle made by the leg and the horizontal is greater than zero.

(l) On the upstroke there is a forward contribution when the angle is less than zero.

(m, n, o) It takes one or more flexible joints to create the conditions for forward impetus throughout most of the kick.

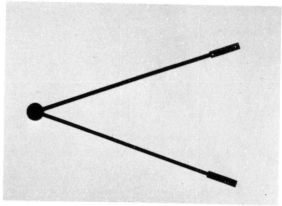

15a

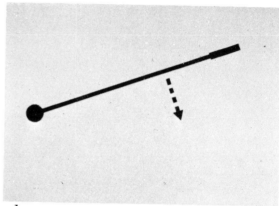

15b

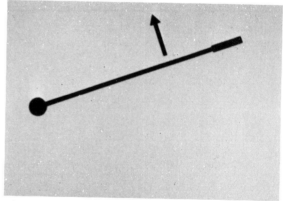

15c

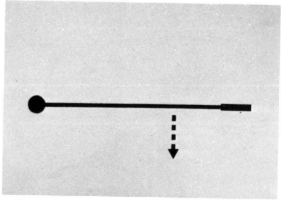

15d

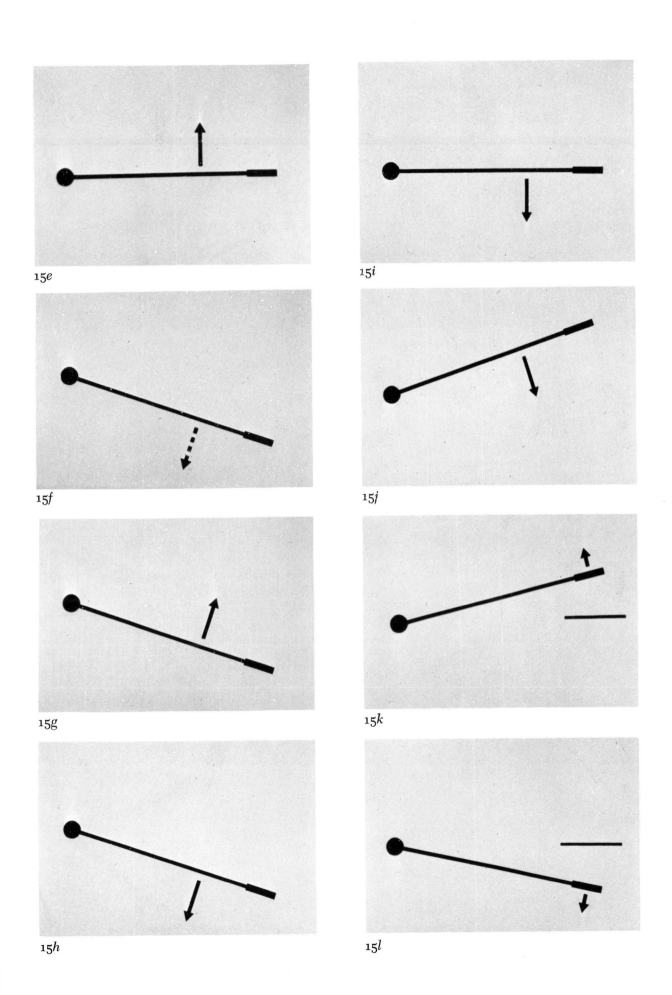

15e

15i

15f

15j

15g

15k

15h

15l

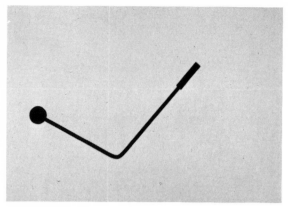

15*m*

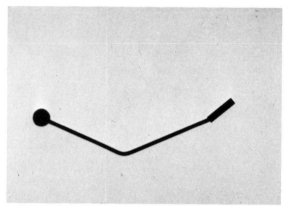

15*n*

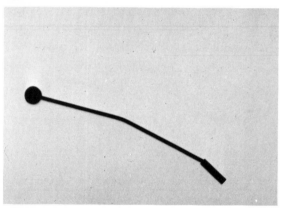

15*o*

16. Leg action is loose, undulating, and whiplike. The goal is to build up great speed of the feet and to have them in the right direction for a backward thrust. Note the excellent ankle flexibility. Photo #1 is highly significant. The bubbles indicate the velocity of the foot in its final downward movement. Compare the positions of the right foot from photo #1 to #2. In photo #2 the upbeat has started and flexion of the foot is the other way. A similar pattern is seen in other photos in the series. If the ankles are loose enough the correct flexion is automatic. Looseness is the key to effective leg action.

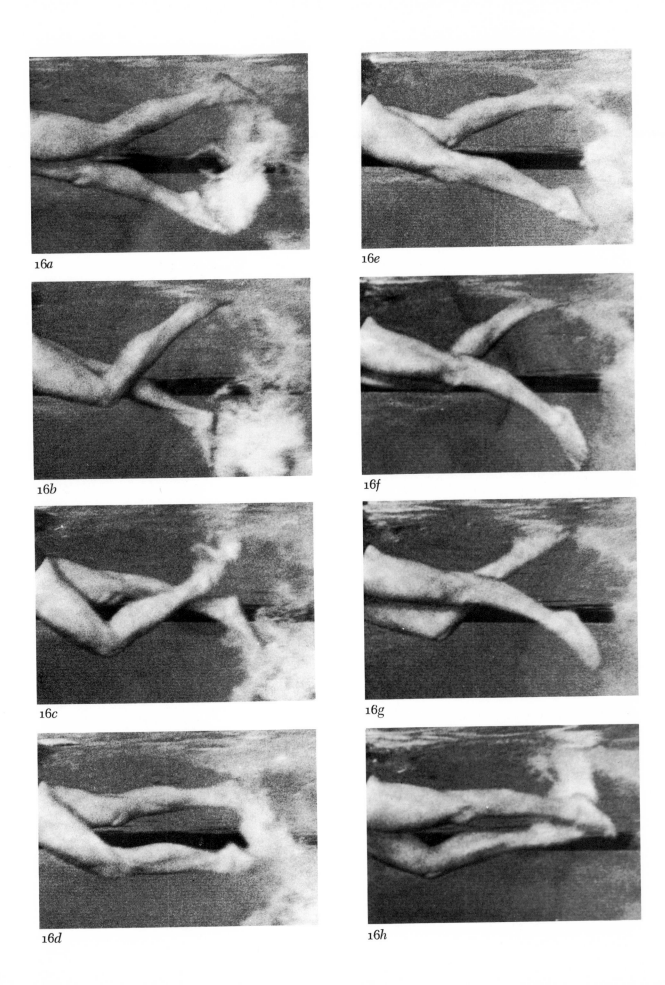

16a

16b

16c

16d

16e

16f

16g

16h

Start

The start has enormous and obvious importance in the sprint race. Where inches often mean victory, you cannot afford anything other than the best start that you can make.

The goals of the start are clear. You want to (1) get away fast, (2) generate a powerful forward thrust, (3) enter the water in such a way as to preserve forward momentum, and (4) establish an initial underwater position that maintains speed.

The toes should curl over the edge of the platform. The grip of the toes helps keep balance and affords a firmer contact for the leg drive. The distance between the feet is about six inches or more—the exact spacing depending on the width of the hips. While waiting for the command, "Take your mark," you want to be relaxed but alert.

At the starter's call of "Take your mark," you bend forward to assume a crouched position. The knees are partially bent. Your arms hang easily. Weight is forward and balanced over the balls of your feet. At the sound of the gun, two main things happen. Your arms begin to swing, and your body moves forward and downward.

Push-off position. A track fan seeing his first swimming meet would be aghast at what would seem an eternity between the sound of the gun and the swimmer actually leaving the platform. He is used to seeing the runner leave the blocks and get underway almost with the sound of the gun. He may wonder why the swimmer doesn't do the same thing. Well, the swimmer could spring at the sound of the gun, but in doing so he would get a most inefficient start. His body position would not be right.

Just before the legs make their final drive the body is stretched out and almost horizontal. At this point, the body's center of gravity is not much higher than the starting platform (photo 2of). You can see the logic of attaining such a position. The job is to drive forward, so the body should be pointed forward. If the final drive were to be made with the body fairly erect, the body would be driven upward rather than forward.

How does the body get into position for the final drive? By gravity! When the gun sounds, you drop your head and flex your ankles. In this way you give up your stable position on the platform and start to fall. You cannot do anything to speed up the falling process. You'll drop at the same rate as any other falling body.

Arms. While you are falling, your arms build up momentum. They have time to do it. The arms swing vigorously upward and complete a full circle. The arms have completed a full cycle and are moving forward just as you are ready to make your final drive from the starting platform. As the arms approach the horizontal they are stopped. The energy developed by the arms is not wasted. This energy is transferred to the body and helps its forward motion.

Entry. When the body enters the water it should be as streamlined as possible. Ideally, the body should form a straight line from the tips of the fingers right through to the toes. There should be no protruding parts. The head is between the arms. The hands enter the water first. The body is held stiff so that the impact of the water does not alter the streamlined position of the body. In summary, a knifelike entry is the goal.

The effectiveness of the start also depends on the angle at which the water is entered. Acquiring the optimum angle takes practice and experience. Too steep an angle of entry would drive you too deep. By the time you reached the surface your competitors would be well on their way. At the other extreme, a very flat dive would dissipate valuable energy against the water.

Glide. After you enter the water you must keep calm and maintain your streamlined body position. In the excitement of a race it's hard to keep in mind that an attempt to start swimming right away can actually slow you down. The initial speed that you develop by driving from a solid surface is greater than swimming speed. It takes patience and experience to hold position until the speed of the glide slows down to swimming speed.

The legs begin their drive first, since their movement interferes less with the streamlining of the body. Initial arm action emphasizes back thrust so that you are not drawn to the surface too soon. The breath is held for several strokes to allow body position to be established.

Attention. You will, of course, be attentive and alert as you await the gun. It's not the time for anyone's mind to wander. However, there are two basic orientations for your attention. You can be concentrating on the sound of the gun or you can be thinking of movement. Research shows that your reaction will be faster if your attention is on what you are going to do.

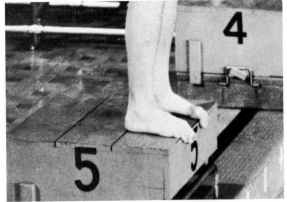

17

18

17. and **18.** The toes are wrapped around the edge of the starting platform.

19. Legs slightly bent. Body weight forward over the balls of the feet.

19

20. (a) "Take your mark" position.
(b) At the gun, arms start to swing. Weight moves forward.
(c) Body falling forward. Arms have picked up speed.
(d, e, f) Body continues to lower and move forward. Legs getting ready to spring.
(g) Arms now being checked. Momentum is transferred to body.
(h) Legs drive as body approaches the horizontal.
(i) Entry.

20a

20b

20c

20d

20e

20f

20g

20h

20i

21. Final leg drive is delayed until the arms and gravity have done their work.

22. Timing among three events—falling forward, arm swing, and leg drive. The arm swing is vigorous and contributes energy. Leg drive is powerful. Note (e) the legs are still coiled to strike. It takes patience. The arms and legs coordinate (f) for an effective forward drive.

21a

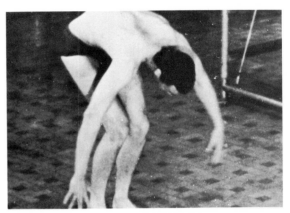

22a

21b

22b

21c

22c

22d

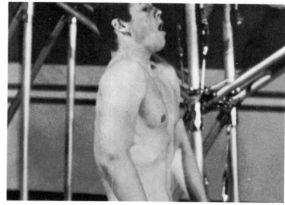

23

22e

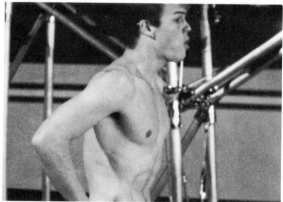

24

23. and **24.** Many swimmers take a series of deep breaths to hyperventilate just before the start.

22f

25. Depth of the dive has to be right. Too deep a dive would lose time and momentum.

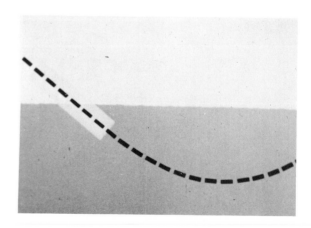

27. Initial speed of the glide is faster than swimming speed. Actual swimming should not start immediately. Wait until speed of glide slows down to swimming speed.

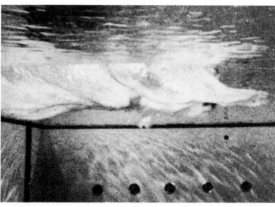

27a

27b

26. Depth of the dive has to be right. A flat dive would dissipate energy.

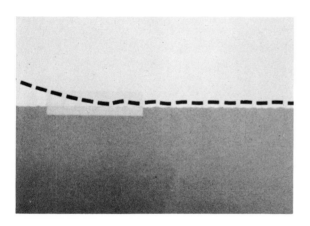

27c

Turn

The turn is a vital part of the race. It must be carried out well. The beginner may regard the turn as an obstacle and almost a nuisance. In contrast, the skilled swimmer sees the turn as an enormous advantage. He knows that the well-executed turn can increase speed and reduce over-all time. The records made in short pools are always faster than those made in long pools. That's because more turns are made in short pools.

The reason that the turn can add speed is that you have a chance to push from a solid surface, the wall of the pool. In addition, during the glide, a rest can be gained.

The task of the turn is to reverse direction and to do so quickly and efficiently. In freestyle swimming the rules no longer require a handtouch. Any part of the body can make contact with the pool wall. Hence for practical purposes there are no restrictions. You can turn almost any way that you want.

The fine sprinter uses some variation of the somersault turn. As he nears the wall, he dives, tucks, and twists. These actions put his legs in position to push against the wall. After the push, he glides and then resumes swimming.

To carry out the first part of the turn you've got to both somersault and twist. Let's consider the somersault. A good somersault really amounts to making an efficient change or transition. In normal swimming you are moving forward with your body level or in horizontal alignment. Your task becomes to destroy this stable, flat position and to spin quickly in the vertical plane.

The way to spin quickly is to create a force that pushes down your upper body and one that lifts your lower body. The movements that bring about these two results are as follows. If you drop your head, the water resistance or drag created by your upper body is greatly increased. The spinning action is started. At the same time you increase the speed of the somersault by creating an upward force on your lower body. You do this by driving downward with both your legs and your hands. The two forces, downward on the upper body and upward on the lower body, combine to speed up the somersault.

You also increase the speed of the somersault by flexing or tucking your body. By making your body compact it spins much easier and faster than if it were stretched out.

Twist. You can see that if you were to do only a somersault (actually, a half somersault), you would push off the wall while on your back. It takes a half twist of your body to put you on your stomach. As you are somersaulting you start twisting. This twisting action brings the legs slightly to one side. The feet leave the water. During the somersault, a quarter twist is enough. As a result of a quarter twist you will be on your side when you are ready to push off the wall. As you drive and start your glide, you make another quarter twist which puts you back in swimming position.

Timing. It's easy to know or recognize good timing of your turn. A well-timed turn will let you end up with your legs in a solid position against the wall. Your legs should have just the right amount of bend when they reach the wall. The optimum amount of leg bend will vary somewhat from swimmer to swimmer.

The key to good timing of the turn is the dive. If you start your dive too soon, you will have to wait and drift toward the pool wall, thus losing valuable time. If you dive too late, you will be cramped and won't have enough room for a good execution of your somersault and twist.

It takes practice and experience to develop reliable judgment as to when to start your dive. You have to work at it. Your judgment has to reach the point where you can start the dive quickly and decisively. Even the expert sometimes mistimes a turn. But even one bad turn can hurt him in a race against other champs. That's why he gives the turn a great deal of practice attention.

Off the wall. Your speed off the wall depends on two factors—the power of your leg drive and the streamlining of your body. You will want a powerful push off the wall. Pushing from a solid surface gives you a chance to develop great speed, and you will want to take full advantage of this opportunity. The leg drive should be an all-out effort.

As you push from the wall the arms are moved forward. The head is between the arms. During the glide the body is held straight. This streamling of the body reduces drag or resistance and thus helps to maintain speed.

As you drive off the wall and glide in a streamlined position, you have about the same situation as you have when you enter the water in the start. Because of the drive afforded by a solid surface, initial body speed is faster than swimming speed. You can see that if you try to swim too soon you will both reduce speed and waste energy. Patience is needed.

The more thoroughly that you understand the turn, the quicker you will master it. You will want to analyze each part of the turn—the dive, somersault, spin, twist, contact with the wall, push, streamlined position, glide, and when to resume swimming. But, of course, you will keep in mind that the parts must blend to make a turn that is decisive, smooth, continuous, and, above all, fast. After all, you are in a race. You can see that an effective turn is going to take understanding, work, and attention.

28a

28b

28c

28. The turn should never be viewed as a nuisance or obstacle. A well-executed turn actually increases swimming speed.

29. All fine sprinters use some form of the somersault turn. The start of the turn must be well timed but fast and decisive.

29a

29b

29c

29d

30c

30. The somersaulting action has started (a and b). Photos c and d show the two main forces at work in spinning the body. The head lowers. The hands and legs push downward. The legs drive off the wall (g and h). The first part of the glide is on the side (i and j). Swimming starts (k) when the speed of the glide slows to swimming speed.

30d

30a

30e

30b

30f

30g

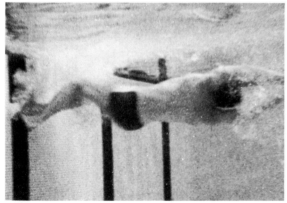

30h

30i

30j

30k

Training

In determining your day-to-day workout programs there is no substitute for an experienced and dedicated coach. Your coach will help you in many ways, but one of his most critical contributions to your success will be the work schedules that he gives you. In designing your programs he can take account of many factors that especially apply to you.

Your coach naturally expects your full cooperation, but he doesn't want you to work blindly. He knows that your enthusiasm will be greater and your progress faster if you understand some of the "whys" of what is being done. In brief, your understanding of conditioning and training methods is not for the purpose of second-guessing your coach. Instead, such an understanding will help you profit more from coaching instruction.

Goals. Your training schedule is designed to accomplish three main goals. You will want to improve techniques including starts and turns. You will want to become faster. And you will want to build great endurance. These three goals are related to each other. Work designed to reach one goal also helps reach the others.

Perfecting technique is an ongoing process. Your form will get continuous attention from you and your coach. You will work especially to ingrain efficient form to the point that it becomes almost instinct. In this way your form will be solid enough to hold up under the conditions of stress and fatigue that you can expect in a race. There is no conflict between working on technique and any other goal. You can and should be conscious of form even if the primary goal of the moment is speed or endurance.

A sprinter must, of course, include lots of speed work in the schedule. In general, speed depends on the amount of power that is developed and the efficiency with which the power is applied. A great deal of fast swimming builds power. At the same time, fast swimming affords practice in carrying out techniques under conditions of high speed.

All training goals are important, but the most significant aspect of modern training methods has been the building of greater endurance. Today's swimmers are much better conditioned than those of a generation ago.

Rationale. Within certain limits the body has a remarkable ability to adjust to the task given to it. This is the basic fact that underlies training and conditioning methods in swimming and other sports.

The word "task" is highly significant. The task given to the body in training depends upon the nature of the event. In addition to specific skills, most sports require both strength and endurance. The ratios of these two factors can vary from one sport to another. There are extremes. For example, in track and field the shot-putter's physical needs contrast with those of the distance runner. The shot-putter is concerned almost entirely with strength. His performance depends on a quick burst of power. At the other end of the scale, the distance runner's ability to perform depends primarily on his endurance. Obviously, the workout goals and therefore schedules of the two athletes will be very different. In planning his training program the shot-putter will give his body the primary task of building great strength. The distance runner's program will be designed to develop great endurance.

Regardless of the task the body must be given a chance to adjust. Both time and spacing are needed. The work load is gradually increased. In other words, the training is "progressive." In this way the body gets used to the task and is able to make the needed changes or adjustments.

Great sprinters are always very strong athletes. That figures, because sprinting requires great power. But the sprinter also needs enormous endurance. In terms of energy output over a time period, a one-hundred-yard swim is about equivalent to running 440 yards.

In recent times all sports where measurement is available have had record explosions. In no sport has the record explosion been more spectacular than in swimming. The "secret" of the explosion has been greatly increased work. There was a time when the swimmer "perfected" his style and then afterward barely practiced between competitions. During the first part of the twentieth century it was discovered that conditioning could bring about enormous advantages. Records started to fall. It became clear that the athlete who worked hard in practice to get in shape performed much better. The famous Yale coach, Bob Kiphuth, was a highly influential pioneer in this effort. Coach Kiphuth's emphasis on the idea of work produced a long series of great Yale teams.

In this half of the twentieth century the need to work hard in practice has been increasingly emphasized. More and more mileage is being swum. Two related scientific efforts have been underway. There is an attempt to find out the optimum amount of practice work and the ways that the work should be carried out so that the body can best profit from it. The first problem still remains somewhat subjective. Experienced coaches are needed to figure out the point at which a swimmer has had the right amount of work. As for applying the "doses" of work, science and trial and error have produced some truly effective methods.

The common denominator of all good workout programs is work itself. But in setting up a specific workout there are infinite possibilities. That's because of the variables that lend themselves to different combinations. There is the distance to be swum, the pace or time, the number of repetitions or times the distance is swum, and the amount of rest taken between repetitions.

Interval Training and Repetition Training. These two terms will become increasingly familiar to you. The methods are somewhat similar, but there are important differences. Both involve the four basic variables that have been mentioned. For example, under either method part of the day's work might be swimming one hundred yards ten times (10 × 100). However, there are two related differences between interval training and repetition training. These differences involve the length of the rest interval between repetitions and usually the speed at which a repetition is swum. Concerning the rest interval, central to interval training is the idea that recovery from the previous repetition should not be complete before doing the next one. Your rest will be very short so that your heart rate will still be fast. In contrast, repetition training calls for a rest interval long enough for almost complete recovery. Heart rate approaches normal, and you breathe without difficulty.

Because repetition training gives you more time to rest between repeats, the repetitions are usually faster than in interval training. In repetition training a portion of the race is selected as the repeat. This section is swum somewhat faster than it would be in the race. The same is seldom true for interval training, because recovery from previous repeats is not complete. To increase the pace in interval training, either the rest intervals would have to be longer or the distance of the repeats shorter.

Both systems, interval training and repetition training, can provide for an infinite variety of workout programs. In addition, there are other methods of training that your coach will prescribe from time to time. Regardless of the methods used you can expect to do a lot of work. The body adjusts, but no more than it has to. The only way it can get used to a lot of work is to do a lot of work.

Land Exercises. Great competitive swimming requires both endurance and strength. The best and most direct way to develop swimming endurance is by doing enough swimming. Interval training, repetition training, and other methods are designed to build endurance. As for strength, however, it was discovered that it can be developed faster by means of land exercises.

Swimmers use a vast variety of exercises. There are literally hundreds in use. Most of them fall into one of four categories—weight training, isometrics, apparatus work, and calisthenics. The basic idea in strength building is to increase gradually the work load of the muscles. The muscles adjust to greater work and become stronger. Systematic increases are essential. The muscles will only adjust to the work given to them.

Nearly all exercises tend to have value. However, weight training offers an important advantage. The resistance of each exercise can be conveniently increased and accurately measured. In this way weight training permits almost optimum schedules.

A general weight-training program can develop all-round strength, but you've got to keep in mind your basic goal—that of becoming a fine swimmer. Under the guidance of your coach you will want to set up a program that is specifically designed to improve swimming. Such a program will emphasize development of the muscles that make the major contributions to propulsion through the water. To build up muscles that add nothing to the swimming effort can actually hamper performance. Endurance can be reduced.

Your coach may prescribe isometric exercises. These are different from other exercises in that the muscles contract without bodily movement. When carried out against an immovable object the amount of resistance cannot be measured. However, isometrics do have some advantages. A critical point in a stroke movement can be isolated and given special attention. Hence isometrics can be used both to build muscle and to aid the learning process.

You don't have to be an expert on land exercises, but the more you understand the importance of this training, the more enthusiasm you will have for it. And the more cooperation you will give your coach.

Kickboard and Leg-tied Drills. Most of the yardage you cover in the pool will be with normal swimming. However, most coaches add two special drills. You will be asked to kick certain distances with a kickboard. Also, you will be asked to swim with your legs tied. When you use a kickboard, your legs supply the entire propulsion, and when you tie your legs, the arms must do all of the work.

Each drill has two basic purposes. In using the kickboard the legs receive more stress than they would in normal swimming. The overload builds strength and endurance. Also the efficiency of leg action receives more attention. The efficiency of this action can be examined and corrections can be made. The same purposes are served by tying the legs. The arms get more work than they ordinarily would, and their action can get special attention.

Picking your event. You may have already gravitated toward the free-style events. Even though this style might be your first preference and your best event, it pays to learn the other three competitive strokes—backstroke, butterfly, and breaststroke. You cannot be sure where your best aptitude lies until you've given each stroke a try. You will get a lot of satisfaction from mastering the other strokes, and there will be times when you can bring in extra points that could mean victory for your team.

You may become either a sprinter or a distance swimmer. But, again, it's best to keep the option open. Experience, especially actual racing, will indicate your most natural distance. When your best distance does become clear your workout schedules will be shaped so as to emphasize either speed or distance.

Warm-up. Great athletes in all sports start each practice session with a thorough warm-up. They wouldn't think of doing otherwise. For some reason the beginner tends to view his warm-up as a mere ritual or nuisance. It takes him a while to realize that the warm-up is an essential part of his workout.

A great variety of warm-up routines can be effective. There is lots of room for experiment. However, for good reasons concerned with human nature the coach's instructions are usually specific. If there are specific things to do, even the novice tends to get an adequate warm-up. Most top swimmers cover about one thousand yards in warming up. They often start with a long swim of about four to five hundred yards. They follow this swim with shorter distances at faster speeds. Brief rests are taken between repeats. Beginners are usually instructed to follow a similar pattern but to swim less yardage.

Getting a warm-up at a large meet can pose some problems. The pool will be crowded, and there will be limited time. You and your coach will probably work out a warm-up routine that will depend heavily on land exercises.

Effect on Your Life. You probably already know that great success takes dedication and sacrifice. You cannot become an outstanding swimmer by taking a few dips in the pool and then doing anything else that you want. It is best to be realistic and know the price of achievement. The price includes discipline and hard work. There is no easy road.

No athlete can get in condition for championship swimming without subjecting himself to almost daily stress. There is no other way to do it. It is human and natural enough to reject punishment and pain. Only the unusual person can persevere to great swimming achievement.

After you accept the price of success, there are still other patterns you must take into consideration. You can surely understand the need to put great stress on your body. You know that's the way that your body becomes efficient and capable of performance. But since you are going to be under this calculated and profitable stress, you cannot also be placed under a lot of other stresses—emotional and otherwise. To the best of your ability you should try to streamline or regulate your life. You cannot afford to waste your energies and time.

The life of a champion has to be Spartan, but in ordering your life and using your time well you do not and should not exclude other worthwhile activities. The discipline that you derive from your training should carry over and help you in other activities. Many great swimmers continue to be honor students throughout college and then go on to distinguished professional or business careers.

You are going to work hard to become a fine swimmer. But you will feel more than rewarded by the joy of competition and the satisfaction of having done well.